TOM O'...
PRESENTS...

THE WORLD'S WORST JOKES

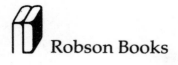

First published in Great Britain in 1991 by
Robson Books Ltd, Bolsover House,
5-6 Clipstone Street, London W1P 7EB

Illustrations by Jim Hutchings
Caricatures by Trevillion

British Library Cataloguing in Publication Data
O'Connor, Tom, 1940–
Tom O'Connor presents the world's worst jokes.
I. Title
828.9140208
ISBN 0 86051 753 5

Typeset by EMS Photosetters, Thorpe Bay, Essex
Printed and bound in Great Britain by W.B.C.
Print Ltd; and W.B.C. Bookbinders Ltd, Mid-
Glamorgan, S. Wales.

Introduction

I never quite understood why the Pestalozzi Children's Village Trust asked *me* to come up with the *World's Worst Jokes* ... but I was glad to be asked and to be able to support such a worthwhile organization.

As you can imagine, for a comedian of my calibre it was easy to think of the worst jokes, but I also asked some celebrity mates for their worst, and have been collecting the others through a series of newspaper articles asking Joe (and Joanna) Public to send theirs in. The response has been tremendous. Hundreds of jokesters sent in their best groaner, far too many to be acknowledged individually, and I've selected the very worst, together with a sprinkling of my own. I would like to say a big thank you to you all: it just goes to prove that everyone loves to laugh – and that people will laugh at *anything*!

The work of the Pestalozzi Children's Village is perhaps best summed up in the village motto: 'Give a man a fish and you feed him for a day. Teach him to fish and you feed him for a lifetime!' Their aim is to give the brightest children from the poorest areas of the world the best education and practical training available. Today dozens of Pestalozzi students have returned home and are sharing their knowledge to help in the development of their own countries, while around 120 more students are learning their skills at Pestalozzi's base in the Sussex countryside.

All the royalties from the sale of this book are going towards the Trust's work, so while you're having a good giggle at some of the whoppers included here, you can pat yourself on the back knowing that you've helped this worthwhile cause.

I hope you enjoy it!

I started telling stories when I was very young. I used to read a lot to myself and I adapted my memory into what is now almost photographic. On a wet playtime at school I used to remember poems and things. This is a vital asset, of course, to a comedian, because you can hear something, remember it and retain it perhaps for two years before you need the actual joke. Here's an example. I was doing a cruise routine and needed a tag, and out of the blue came a gag I'd heard eighteen months earlier, and it's the one about the feller who says to the captain of an ocean-going liner, 'It's a nice ship this, isn't it? Are you happy with it?' And the captain says, 'Yes, every man on this ship has been hand-picked. You see the fellow there swabbing the deck – I'd trust him with my life.' And just then a huge wave came and washed this feller over-board, and the passenger said, 'You know that feller you'd trust with your life – he's just cleared off with your mop and bucket.'

Why did the boy call his dog 'Sandwich'?
Because it was half bred.

What do you call five bottles of lemonade?
A pop group.

What drinks do you get at a ghosts' party?
Spirits.

A man went into the baker's for some doughnuts. The baker said, 'I've given up making doughnuts. I'm fed up with the hole business.'

What's a cannibal's favourite meal?
Snake and pygmy pie!

When is a baked potato rude?
When you take off its jacket.

How do you get freckles?
Sunbathe under a sieve.

How do you help a lemon in distress?
Give it lemon-ade.

How do you make a Swiss roll?
Push him down a hill.

What's wet and comes out of a bottle at 100mph?

An Aston Martini.

When I started out I was a singer. Then I found out that the comedians were earning three times the money, so I changed horses. Unfortunately, I started off telling jokes which I soon realized everybody else had heard as well. So I started to avoid the set-piece joke – I'm talking about the sixties now – like 'My brother's a member of the dole protection society. You pay sixpence a week, and if the dole finds you a job these fellers fight your case.' Gradually I realized that this kind of joke, apart from having been heard by everyone, didn't lend itself to any particular style. The first and foremost thing I learned in comedy is that you have to find a style that suits you.

I'll never forget, I was doing a place in Manchester, and it was a very rough club, and for some reason I had to get a grip of the audience and I started to get cocky. Of course, that's the second thing you learn about show-business – never get overwhelmed by your own prowess. I started doing gags like, 'I hope you've enjoyed your meal. The chef's got over his rash . . . I'm only joking, but have you been in the kitchen? Five million flies can't be wrong.' And that was treated to entire silence, because it turned out that there had been an outbreak of food poisoning the week before and two hundred people had been rushed to hospital!

Why did the chewing gum cross the road?
Because it was stuck to the chicken's foot.

Jeremy Irons

What's a vampire's favourite lunch?

Ghoulash!

What do you get if you cross a plate of stew with a cowboy?

Hopalong casserole!

Who has friends for dinner?

A cannibal!

Why did the banana split?

Because it saw the milk shake!

Knock, knock.

Who's there?

Hosanna.

Hosanna who?

Hosanna Claus gets down the chimney I'll never know.

Knock! Knock!

Knock, knock.

Who's there?

You.

You who?

Did you call?

Knock, knock.

Who's there?

Cook.

Cook who?

That's the first one I've heard this year!

Knock, knock.

Who's there?

Carmen.

Carmen who?

Carmen see for yourself.

Knock, knock.

Who's there?

Noah.

Noah who?

Noah good place to eat?

Knock, knock.

Who's there?

Ifor.

Ifor who?

Ifor got my key.

Knock, knock.

Who's there?

Denver.

Denver who?

Denver the good old days.

Knock, knock.

Who's there?

Jupiter.

Jupiter who?

Jupiter fly in my soup?

What's pink and white and travels at 30mph?

A bus-driver's ham sandwich.

What's long and orange and shoots out of the ground at 100mph?

An E-type carrot.

What's round, white and giggles?

A tickled onion.

What's the difference between a mouldy lettuce and a dismal song?

One's bad salad and the other's a sad ballad.

What's the difference between an elephant and a biscuit?

Have you ever tried dunking an elephant in your tea?

What do you get if you cross a hamburger with a Scotsman?

A big Mac.

Two sausages are in a frying pan – one says to the other, 'Cor, it's hot in here.'
    The other one says, 'Blimey, a talking sausage.'

Why did they throw the egg over the wall?
Because it was a chucky egg!!!

Gazza

Why did the tomato go red?

He saw the salad dressing.

What did one tomato say to the other tomato?

You run on and I will ketchup.

What's yellow, then green, then yellow, then green?

A banana that works part-time as a cucumber.

Ben was busy making a pizza. He shouted to his friend, 'Get the dough, I'll knead it soon.'

What is yellow and wet?
A banana in the rain.

What did the egg say?

Nothing – eggs can't speak.

What do witches eat for breakfast?

Snap, crackle and pop!

What sits in a pram and wobbles?

A jelly baby.

What kind of cheese is made backwards?

EDAM.

What do you get if you cross a citrus fruit with a bell?

An orange that 'peals' itself.

What did the orange squash say when the water was poured in his glass?

I'm diluted to meet you.

What does the Queen do when she burps?

She issues a Royal pardon.

Gyles Brandreth

What is 300 metres tall and wobbles?

The trifle tower.

What's little, round and able to lift heavy weights?

An extra strong mint.

What sits in the fruit bowl and shouts for help?

A damson in distress.

When the Israeli army won the Six Day War, one of their secrets was a front line regiment made up of doctors, solicitors and estate agents and, by God, when they said 'Charge', could they charge!

Three blokes were captured by a cannibal tribe in the middle of Africa and they were paraded in front of the Chief. The Chief said, 'You have all got very good skins. You are going to make very good canoes. Before you are killed you can all have one last request.'

The Englishman said, 'I will have a pint of English beer.'

He drank the beer.

The Scotsman said, 'I will have a large Scotch whisky.'

So they gave him a Scotch whisky.

The Irishman said, 'I will have a fork please.'

They said, 'What?'

He said, 'I will have a table fork.'

They gave him a fork and he started poking it in his body all over the place and said, 'You're not going to make a canoe out of me.'

The centenarian was asked by the reporter for the secret of his long life. 'I have never taken strong liquor, never gambled and never played around with women.'

Suddenly from the next room there was a resounding crash and a female scream. 'What in heaven's name was that?' asked the reporter.

'It's my father,' said the old man. 'He's just back from the casino, drunk as a lord, and he's chasing the maid again.'

Man in a chemist: I'd like some rat poison.
Chemist: Have you tried Boots?
Man: Listen, I want to poison them, not kick them to death.

A father was having problems with a little boy who couldn't stop swearing. He was talking to a friend of his in a pub and the friend said, 'What the child needs is a shock. You want to shock him into stopping his foul language. Tell him Santa Claus is going to give him a real surprise for Christmas.' So the night before Christmas he was loading up all the stockings and in the little girl's stocking he put all kinds of things like Barbie dolls, sweeties and what-have-you. In the little boy's stocking he just put two shovelfuls of horse manure.

The next morning the little girl got up and said, 'Look at all the things I have got', and she ran into her brother's room and he was stamping about. She said, 'I have got a Barbie Doll and sweeties and everything. What have you got?'

And the little boy said, 'I've got a horse, but I can't find it.'

Did you hear about the man who asked for a return ticket at the railway station. When they asked him 'where to?', he said, 'Back here, of course.'

'I say, old chap, where did you get that accent?'
  'Eton, old sausage.'
  'Well, I'd give up eatin' old sausage if I were you.'

Why didn't the millionaire have any bathrooms in his mansion?

Because he was filthy rich.

Did you hear about the human cannonball?

He got fired.

1st Cannibal: I don't like your friend.
2nd Cannibal: Well, just eat your vegetables then.

Boy: My sister married an Irishman.
Girl: Oh, really?
Boy: No, O'Connor.

What do you call someone who used to be interested in tractors?

An extractor fan.

Why did the man cross the road a
hundred times?

*Because his braces were caught on the
lamp post.*

How do you tell the difference between two Spanish firemen?

Call them Hose A and Hose B!

Michael Fish

Sue: I can't go to cookery classes any more.
Mum: Why not?
Sue: I burnt something.
Mum: What did you burn?
Sue: The school cookery room.

What's Kylie Minogue's favourite eating place?

Jason's Dona-van.

Mum, now that I'm fifteen, can I wear makeup and pluck my eyebrows?

No, James, you may not!

Why did the teacher go cross-eyed?
He couldn't control his pupils.

Teacher: You missed school yesterday, didn't you, Laura?
Laura: Not much, Miss!

Accountant: Do you want to hear the good news first, or the bad news?
Client: Tell me the good news!
Accountant: I can account for every penny!
Client: What's the bad news?
Accountant: I'm not too sure about the pounds.

The manager of the local department store rang Mr Bloggs.

'It's about your wife,' he said. 'She's been coming in here for the last few days, buying all sorts of things and then offering to pay in milk-bottle tops. I've let her so far, because she's always been a good customer, but now I'm getting rather worried.'

'Now don't you worry,' said Mr Bloggs. 'She's not been well lately. Just let her have what she wants and I'll come in and settle up with you at the end of the month.'

The manager agreed and, for the rest of the month, Mrs Bloggs came to the shop, bought piles of goods and was allowed to pay in milk-bottle tops. Mr Bloggs duly turned up at the end of the month to pay for everything.

'What's the damage?' he asked.
'£658.73p,' said the manager.
'No problem,' said Mr Bloggs. 'Do you
have change for this dustbin lid?'

An Irish feller volunteered to kidnap Rommel when things were not going well in the desert. He said, 'Leave it to me, O'Rafferty has never lost his man yet, just dress me up as an Arab and leave it to me.'

Off he went into the desert fully equipped as an Arab and about two days later there came a telegram saying, 'Rommel Captured.'

There was great delight on the British side, Montgomery gave a great big champagne party and about three days later a very bedraggled O'Rafferty arrived back and they said, 'Congratulations, we're going to give you the Military Medal. What a marvellous feat.'

O'Rafferty said, 'What marvellous feat?'

They said, 'Yes, we got the telegram saying Rommel Captured.'

He said, 'Oh the feller must be dyslexic, the message I sent was "Camel Ruptured".'

Two blokes were in a pub and one said to the other, 'Do you want to buy an elephant for £300?'

The other said, 'Blimey, I've only got a one-bedroom flat, where would I put an elephant?'

The first bloke said, 'Well, how about two for £400?'

And the other said, 'Ah, now you're talking.'

The artist kissed his model tenderly.

'Do you know,' he said, 'you are the first model I've ever kissed?'

'I don't believe you,' she replied. 'How many models have you had?'

'Let's see,' said the artist. 'A bowl of fruit, a basket of dried flowers, a puppy . . . .'

A little boy got a package from his great aunt Gladys.

It read: 'Dear Johnnie, I am sending you another wellington as I heard you've grown another foot.'

Two fellers walking past a cemetery and there was a stone on which it said, 'Here lies a Solicitor and an honest man.'

One said to the other, 'Look they've put two people in the same grave.'

Vic: My wife is going on holiday soon.
Bob: Really, where is she going?
Vic: Alaska.
Bob: Oh, that's okay, I'll ask her myself.

Tony's father said to him, 'Tell your teacher that your mum has just had twins – you might get the day off school if you're lucky.' Tony came home smiling from school. 'Did you tell your teacher about your twin sisters?' his dad asked.

'No, I just told her I had one baby sister, I'm saving the other one for next week!'

Why is a farmer cruel?

Because he pulls the corn by its ears.

Two little boys in the playground, and one says to the other, 'Are you 6 or 4?'

His mate says, 'I don't know.'

The first one says, 'Well, do women worry you?'

He says, 'No.'

'Oh,' he says, 'You're about 4.'

How do witches on broomsticks drink their tea?

Out of flying saucers.

Teacher: What did you do at the weekend, Anne?

Anne: I done me shopping.

Teacher: Done! What about your grammar?

Anne: She done 'er own shopping, Miss.

What did the cannibal say when he saw
the sleeping missionary?

'Oh look! Breakfast in bed!'

What makes a bad joke funny? Sometimes, you need to be familiar with the psychology of the British public. I'll give you an example. There's an old gag which, even when told properly isn't that brilliant – it's the one about the feller driving the wrong way up a one-way street and the policeman says, 'You're driving up a one-way street the wrong way. Didn't you see the arrows?' And the bloke says, 'I didn't even see the Indians.' Now, I've seen a bloke called Bobby Bragg, who's a very funny little comic, he used to be our warm-up man at the BBC, and he does the gag back to front and gets three laughs out of it. Now, why he does it I don't know. He says, 'The feller is going up a one-way street, and the policeman says, "Didn't you see the Indians?"' and everyone laughs nervously because they know he's got it wrong. Then he says, 'No, I didn't even see the arrows.' And they laugh again politely because they realize he's completed the joke but it still ain't funny. And then, off stage, he says in a loud whisper, 'I don't think they've noticed.' That brings the house down.

Batty Books

How to Scare People by Don Dewdat

How to Avoid the Sin of Pride by Hugh Millity

Time to Eat by Dean R Bell

Spying Can be Fun by M I Fife

One Hundred Famous Prayers by Neil Downe

Nuclear Physics Made Easy by Ray D Hayshun

One Hundred Fantastic Premonitions by Hugh Mark Mywerds

Stress is Dangerous by Dickie Hart

Easy Money by Robin Banks

Dinner for Two by Carmen Geddit

Positive Thinking by Hope N Pray

What do you call a man with leaves in his shoes?

Russell.

What do you call a man with a seagull on his head?

Cliff.

What do you call a man with a piece of wood on his head?

Edward.

A little boy in the Grotto saw Father Christmas, and went up to him and kicked him right in the shins and said, 'That's for last year.'

A man looked out and saw a dustman whistling and carrying twelve dustbins all at once. He said, 'That's amazing, how do you do that?'

The dustman said, 'It's easy, I just put my lips together and blow.'

A man was in hospital and every bone in his hand was broken.
He said, 'Doctor, when my hand is better, will I be able to play the piano?'

The doctor said, 'Yes of course you will.'

He said, 'Great, because I never could before.'

A criminal walked into a bank and said, 'This is a muck up.'

They said, 'Don't you mean a stick up?'

'No, I've forgotten my gun.'

What did Chief Running Water call his two sons?

Hot and Cold.

The cannibal was walking through the jungle when he came across a missionary. He said, 'Now, Mr Missionary, what's the best way to eat you? Boiled or roasted?'

'Well actually,' said the missionary, 'I'm a friar.'

One kipper said to the other, 'Smoking's bad for you.'

'It's all right, I've been cured.'

What do you call a secret agent who lives in a bottle of washing up liquid?

Bubble 07.

I enjoy sporting jokes. One of my favourites is about two blokes – a vicar and one of his parishioners – going to a football match. As they're getting near the ground they can hear the tannoy blaring music, and it's all pop. And the vicar says, 'I'm always surprised that they don't play Brahms.' And the other feller says, 'Maybe it's because of the wet grounds.'

There's also the one about two fellers in a queue for a football match, and there's a massive sway of people queuing to get in, and the police horses are trying to cordon the crowd off into lines, and one feller says, 'All this pushing and shoving, you'd think they'd let the horses in first.'

In the days of old variety theatres there were two old ladies watching a show. Listening to a violinist, one said to the other, 'That's a lovely piece of music, I wonder what it is?'

The other said, 'I don't know but there's a card on the stage which will probably say what it is – I'll look.'

So she went off to take a look. When she came back her friend asked, 'What was its title?'

'It's called "Refrain from spitting!' she replied.

What do you give a deaf fisherman?

A herring aid.

What is grey, Italian and conducts an orchestra?

Tusker-nini.

Did you hear about the man who jumped off the Telecom Tower?

He made a hit in the West End.

What do you call a man with no arms and no legs swimming the Channel?
Bob!

Suzanne Dando

The Israeli infantry dug in in the front line and the Arabs were coming at them down the hill. There was a great burst of fire and suddenly a sergeant from the Jewish side shouted, 'Keep still, please, this ammunition costs money.'

What do you call a man with no arms and no legs hanging on a wall?

Art.

What do you call a man with no arms and no legs in a hole in the ground?

Doug.

What do you call a man with a red blob on his face?

Mark.

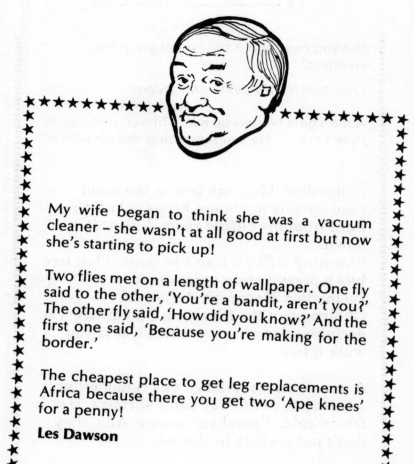

My wife began to think she was a vacuum cleaner – she wasn't at all good at first but now she's starting to pick up!

Two flies met on a length of wallpaper. One fly said to the other, 'You're a bandit, aren't you?' The other fly said, 'How did you know?' And the first one said, 'Because you're making for the border.'

The cheapest place to get leg replacements is Africa because there you get two 'Ape knees' for a penny!

Les Dawson

Why did the farmer drive a steam roller over the field of potatoes?

Because he liked mashed potatoes with his dinner.

Did you hear about the cannibals at the wedding?

They toasted the bride and groom.

A man gets beaten up every fifteen minutes in New York . . . He's getting really fed up with it!

Councillor: That oak tree in the main road outside my house keeps out all the light from my sitting room. I want it down.
Planning Officer: Can't be done. That tree has a preservation order on it.
Councillor: Never mind that. As Chairman of the Planning Committee, I'll declare it dangerous – which it is if you walk into it.

A pensioner on holiday was considering whether or not to buy some shrimps. Her friend said, 'Spend yer money, Ada, they don't put pockets in shrouds.'

This bloke gets married and he says to his new mother-in-law, 'I want you to think of my house as your house.'

A week later she sold it!

What drink do estate agents prefer?

Proper tea.

Hear about the cannibal that joined the police force? He said he wanted to grill the suspects.

Fred to Joe who had just returned from a trip to Blackpool: 'Did yer goo on a donkey?'
Joe: 'No ah day, ah went on a train from Dudley Port.'

Why did the little boy take a ruler to bed?

Because he wanted to see how long he had been asleep.

Station announcement: The train now arriving at platforms, 2, 3, 4, 5, 6, 7, 8, 9 and 10 is coming in sideways.

What do smelly farmers wear?

Dung-arees.

Do you know what happened to the crook who stole the calendar?

He got twelve months.

Did you hear about the worker in the banana-packing company?

He got the sack for throwing the bent ones away.

What do spotty people go riding in?

Acne carriages.

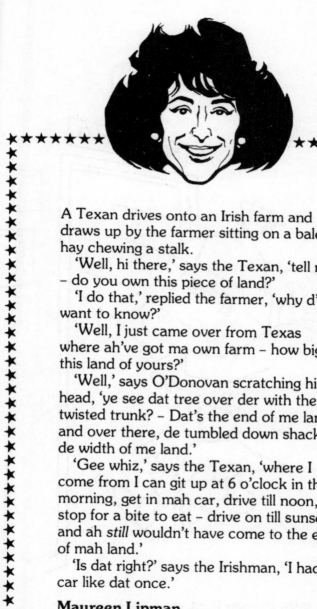

A Texan drives onto an Irish farm and draws up by the farmer sitting on a bale of hay chewing a stalk.

'Well, hi there,' says the Texan, 'tell me – do you own this piece of land?'

'I do that,' replied the farmer, 'why d'ye want to know?'

'Well, I just came over from Texas where ah've got ma own farm – how big is this land of yours?'

'Well,' says O'Donovan scratching his head, 'ye see dat tree over der with the twisted trunk? – Dat's the end of me land and over there, de tumbled down shack is de width of me land.'

'Gee whiz,' says the Texan, 'where I come from I can git up at 6 o'clock in the morning, get in mah car, drive till noon, stop for a bite to eat – drive on till sunset and ah *still* wouldn't have come to the end of mah land.'

'Is dat right?' says the Irishman, 'I had a car like dat once.'

Maureen Lipman

Who gets the sack as soon as he starts work?

The postman.

Two Scotsmen are brought up for being drunk and incapable, and the judge says, 'How do you know they were drunk and incapable?' and the policeman says, 'Well, the fellow on the right had his wallet open and was throwing money away, and the fellow on the left was giving it back.'

David: How do you keep a twit waiting?
John: How?
David: I'll tell you tomorrow.

What do Eskimos sing at coming of age parties?

Freeze a jolly good fellow.

What does a vampire take when he has a cold?

Coffin drops.

A little old bloke goes into the bookmaker's shop and says, 'It's my birthday today, I'm 82 and I want to put all my life savings on Red Giant in the 3 o'clock race.'

The bookmaker says, 'Listen, Grandad, don't do it, for me, Red Giant is a donkey, he has only got three legs, he's hopeless, he runs to the right all the time and he hasn't got a chance, it's 300 to 1. Don't back it.'

The old man says, 'Listen, it's my birthday, I can do what I like, I am going to back it. £10,000 on Red Giant at 300 to 1.'

The bookmaker's thinking, 'My God, this old feller, it's his life savings, what happens if he stays in my shop and hears this and loses all his money. He'll have a heart attack and fall down in my shop.' So he rings up the blower man at the course, the feller who gives the commentary, and he says, 'Listen, Charlie. When you're giving the commentary can you pretend that Red Giant has got a bit of a chance?'

Charlie says, 'Don't worry, Harry, leave it to me.'

So the commentary came over and he says, 'It's the 3 o'clock race from Haymarket, the horses are at the start and they're off. They're coming up to the first fence now and Red Giant's tongue is hanging out and he's still there. Well, they're all over the first and coming to the second and Red Giant is puffing and blowing, and running to the right, but he's still there.'

Then there's a break in transmission of about one and a half minutes and suddenly this voice comes screaming back over the tannoy, 'And they're over the last fence now and Red Giant is 36 lengths clear and I'm not kidding, Harry. I'm not kidding.'

Maurice had seen off his wife for a holiday with her sister.
Friend: 'How's you getting on without the missis?'
Maurice: 'Fine, but for the fust couple of hours after her'd gone I thought I'd gone deaf.'

A woman was crying whilst looking at a blank piece of paper and her friend asked her what the matter was. She said, 'It's a letter from my son – he knows we can't read and we know he can't write, but it's lovely to hear from him anyway.

Henry Cooper OBE KSG

What did the corpse say as he was being lowered into the wrong hole by the undertaker?

You're making a grave mistake.

When was the little boy a magician?

When he walked down the road and turned into a sweet shop.

'My doctor told me to take two of these pills on an empty stomach.'
'Did they do any good?'
'I don't know. They kept rolling off in the night.'

A man was in court for stealing a car. He said, 'I didn't steal it, my Lord. It was parked outside the cemetery and I thought the owner was dead.'

There were twelve copy cats, one fell off his chair, how many were left?
None!

Where do policemen live?
999 Letsbe Avenue.

What time did the man go to the dentist?
Two-thirty.

What's the cannibal's favourite game?
Swallow my leader.

Why did the cowboy die with his boots on?

Because he knew he'd stub his toes when he kicked the bucket.

Who earns a living by driving customers away?

A taxi-driver.

Tim: Did you hear about Charlie Jones?
Jim: No.
Tim: He invested all his savings into a paper shop.
Jim: Well, what happened?
Tim: It blew away.

A soccer fan was sitting in the corner of the pub crying into his ale. At that moment his pal walked in and asked, 'What's wrong with you, Jim?'

'You might well ask me what's wrong,' he sobbed. 'You might well ask . . .'

'What's wrong then?'

'Don't ask me. It's all right for you, lad. I came off nights and found the wife had run off with the feller from next door . . . The two kids have run away to sea . . . When I got back from the pub this morning the house had burned down . . . And Liverpool lost.'

'Come on, don't upset yourself.'

'Upset meself?' he choked. 'I can't understand it. They were winning at half-time.'

A feller rang up Somerset House and said, 'I believe you have records that go back hundreds of years?'

They said, 'That's right.'

He said, 'Well, can you play me Bill Haley's "Rock Around the Clock"?'

What do you call a man with three pieces of wood on his head?

Edward Woodward.

What do you get if you cross an Egyptian mummy with a motor mechanic?

Toot and Carman.

What did Noah use to see in the dark?

Floodlights.

Where do snowmen go to dance?
A snowball.

The psychiatrist and his patient were sitting in his office.

'Now tell me, Mrs Bell, why have your family sent you to me for treatment?'

'It's only because of my passion for pizzas,' said Mrs Bell. 'Just because I'm fond of them, they think there's something wrong with me.'

'That's ridiculous,' said the psychiatrist. 'I'm fond of pizzas myself.'

'Really,' said Mrs Bell. 'Then you *must* come and visit me. I've got a whole shed full of them.'

How did the waitress get an electric shock?

She stood on a bun and a currant ran up her leg.

Teacher to little boy: Where are the Andes?
On the end of my wristies.

An Irishman went into a car lot looking to buy a car.

'I want to buy a car,' said Murphy.

'I've got just what you're looking for,' said the salesman. 'There's a special offer on this car here – it's just £200.'

'But it's got no doors!' exclaimed Murphy.

'That's why it's just £200,' said the salesman.

'Yeah, but how am I going to get in it?' cried Murphy.

What's old and wrinkled and belongs to Grandad?

Grandma.

In the days when milk was delivered from the churn, Mary-Ann suspected that her milkman was serving her with a watered down product. To make her point she went to him one day with two jugs and said, 'I'll have a half pint of milk in this one and half a pint of water in this and I'll mix me own.'

Why did the little boy take the pencil to bed?

Because he wanted to draw the curtains.

Why is a chef cruel?

He whips the cream and beats the eggs.

How did Quasimodo know when the end was near?

He had a hunch.

A bloke went into the bank and said to the cashier, 'I would like to take out a loan.'
And the cashier said, 'Terribly sorry, but the Loan Arranger is not in today.'
So he said, 'Can I speak to Tonto then?'

What do you call a Cockney girl with a plate of fried eggs on her head?

Caff.

What do you call an Arab with a piece of ham on his head?

Hamed.

What do you call an Arab with two pieces of ham on his head?

Mohamed.

Why are archaeologists so sad?

Their careers are in ruins.

Why did the policeman climb the tree?

He was a member of the Special Branch.

★★★★★★★★★★★★★★★★★★★★★★★★★★★

Edwina Currie received a greetings card from Sammy Davis Junior and Ella Fitzgerald. The note inside said: Happy Christmas from Sam 'n' Ella!

Frank Carson

★★★★★★★★★★★★★★★★★★★★★★★★★★★★★★★★★

'I'm going to have to report you, sir,' said the policeman to the speeding driver. 'You were doing eighty-three miles an hour.'

'Nonsense, officer,' replied the driver. 'I've only been in the car for five minutes!'

Why didn't the man who invented electricity make a lot of money?

Because someone else invented the meter.

Did you hear about the woman who made herself a pair of trousers out of £50 notes? She ended up sitting on a fortune.

Did you hear about the lion that became a cannibal?

He had to swallow his pride.

Gags have certainly changed since I first started. I suppose my early days at the clubs in 1964/5, there weren't as many comedians *per se* as there are today. What we did have was a whole glut of nightclub compères who could sing very well and who learned about six or eight extremely off-colour jokes. They were billing themselves as comedy entertainers, with the back-up, of course, that if the gags were dying, then they could sing. A lot of the gags in those days were racial. A lot of them were extremely – well, they used an awful lot of language in those days. Everything was a little bit tacky in those days, though there are some very good comedians from that era, real experts. Bernard Manning is one for a start. As well as being known as extremely blue, he can be the best teller of a clean story in Britain, without doubt. I used to love the one of Bernard's where he says, 'Julius Caesar was leading his armies across Britain, and they came across this particular field where he decided to fight his next battle, and he turned around and shouted, "Halt!" Twenty thousand legionnaires stopped and they could hear this scuffling coming from the back. Eventually this little bloke with a bow and arrow in his hand came up, and Caesar said, "What are you doing? I said Halt." And the feller said, "I thought you said Walt."'

Visitor: I wonder what that lion would say if it could speak?
Zookeeper: It would probably say, 'Excuse me sir, but I'm a tiger.'

A man and his dog were playing draughts, and the dog won. A chap who was watching said, 'My word, what an amazing dog. He could make you a fortune.'

'No,' said the man, 'He's not that good. I've beaten him once or twice.'

A man went to the optician, and the optician took him over to the card on the wall. He said, 'Can you read this line of letters?'

The man said, 'No.'

Then he moved to the line above, which had bigger letters. He said, 'Can you read that?'

The man said, 'No.'

Then he pointed to the biggest line. He said, 'Can you read this?'

The man said, 'No.'

The optician said, 'This is serious!'

The man said, 'I know, I can't read.'

What did the ghost teacher say to her kids?

'Watch the board and I'll go through it again.'

I always enjoy the gag about the little boy who is painting, and the teacher comes up and says, 'What are you doing?' He says, 'I'm painting God.' The teacher says, 'Nobody knows what God looks like,' and he says, 'They will when I've finished.'

Speaking of teachers, there's a really good apocryphal story which I got from a headmaster. It's the school nativity play where the four- and five-year-olds are performing, and everything's fine until the mothers arrive – because mums and dads can be very off-putting when the children see them in the audience. So you've got Mary and Joseph who come up and knock on the inn door, the innkeeper opens the door and immediately he sees his mum and dad in the front row and forgets what he has to say. And Joseph says, 'May we stay here for the night?' and the innkeeper says, 'Clear off, we're chocker.' And Joseph panics, then he forgets his lines and says, 'But my wife's having a baby.' And the innkeeper says, 'Well it's not my fault your wife's having a baby.' And Joseph says, 'No, and if you read the Bible you'll find it's not my fault either.'

Why should you never shave a man with a wooden leg?

Because a razor's much better.

One day a woman was walking down the sea shore, admiring the view, when she spotted a man thrashing around in the water, drowning.
    'I can't swim! I can't swim!' shouted the man.
    'So what?' replied the woman, 'I can't play the piano but I don't go round shouting about it.'

Two men were talking and one said he'd seen a yacht race on holiday. And one yacht did a foul and everybody mooed.
    'Don't you mean "booed",' said the other.
    'No, it was Cowes week.'

A man and wife were at the airport going on holiday. They had loads and loads of luggage and the man said to his wife, 'Dear, I wish we had brought the piano along as well.'
    She said, 'Why's that?'
    He said, 'I left the tickets on the lid.'

Hear about the man who had three daughters, called Hazel, Coco and Brazil?

They were all nuts.

Two mind readers. One said to the other, 'You're all right, how am I?'

Dentist: Stop waving your arms about and making faces. I haven't even touched you yet.
Patient: I know, but you're standing on my foot.

What about the phone call at the hospital, and the matron said, 'Hello?' and a voice said, 'I'm enquiring about the gentleman in Ward A, could you tell me how he is?' She said, 'Yes, he's very comfortable, he's having his operation tomorrow. Who's speaking?' And the feller said, 'It's the bloke in Ward A here, nobody tells me anything.'

Two men in a pub:
'My ambition is to run my own pub. What's yours?'
'Thanks, I'll have a pint of cider!'

Being bald isn't all it's cracked up toupee. . . .

How do vampires travel across the sea?
In blood vessels.

A man was disqualified from a walking race because he won it two years running.

At an elegant cocktail party one of the guests suddenly let out a great big burp, which reverberated around the whole room. The host was horrified. 'You there,' he cried, 'how dare you burp in front of my wife?'

'Oh sorry,' said the guest, 'I didn't know it was her turn.'

Policeman: When I saw you driving down the road I thought to myself 'Fifty-five at least.'
Motorist: Well, that not quite fair. I think this hat makes me look older.

Joan: My husband got a bad sprain at football last week.
Jean: I didn't know he played.
Joan: He doesn't. It was his larynx he sprained.

Doctor, doctor, I have a split personality. I keep thinking there are two of me.

Could you repeat that? And this time don't both speak at once.

Doctor, doctor, I feel like a pair of curtains.

Pull yourself together, man.

What do you call two thieves?

A pair of nickers.

The dentist was sworn in at court. 'Do you swear to tell the tooth, the whole tooth and nothing but the tooth?'

What do you call a cowboy with no money?

Skint Eastwood.

What did Dick Turpin say after he'd ridden Black Bess all the way to York?

'Whoa there.'

A man phones his friend and says 'How are things?'

His friend says, 'Incredible. Profits in the business are up three hundred per cent. I just won a quarter of a million pounds on the pools. My daughter graduated from Cambridge University with First Class Honours. My wife's oil paintings have just been accepted for one of the top galleries in London.'

The man said to his friend, 'I didn't realise you had someone with you. I'll call you back.'

Michael Winner

Doctor: Face the window, would you?
Now stick out your tongue?
Patient: Why do I have to face the
window?
Doctor: Because I don't like the man next
door.

On a busy motorway some traffic
policemen drew up alongside a lady who
was knitting as she was driving.
'Pullover,' they shouted.
  'No, a pair of socks,' she said.

Doctor, doctor, my husband thinks he's a chicken.
You must take him to a specialist right away.
I would but we need the eggs.

Doctor, doctor, my son thinks he's a television set.
Don't worry, we'll soon cure him of that.
But I don't want him cured – I just want him adjusted so I can get Channel 4!

Doctor, doctor, I keep thinking I'm a bell.
Take some of these and if you don't feel any better give me a ring.

Doctor, doctor, I'm having terrible trouble with my breathing.
Take a seat, Ms Jones, and we'll see if we can put a stop to that.

The man went into the doctors and said, 'Doctor, my eyes are bad.'
The doctor replied, 'Be like a rabbit, eat carrots.'
A few weeks later the man went back. The doctor asked, 'Eyes better?'
The man said, 'Yes, but now I keep tripping over my ears.'

Doctor, doctor, I can't stop stealing things.
I'll give you something to take.

Doctor, doctor, I feel like a pack of cards.

Wait here – I'll deal with you later.

Patient: I keep thinking I'm a dog.
Doctor: How long have you felt like this?
Patient: Ever since I was a puppy.

Doctor, doctor, I keep thinking I'm a bridge.
What's come over you?
Four cars, two lorries and five buses.

Doctor, doctor, I feel like a billiard ball.

Stop pushing in and get to the end of the queue.

Doctor: You need glasses.
Patient: That's brilliant, how did you know?
Doctor: I could tell as soon as you walked through the window.

Doctor, doctor, my wife thinks she's a duck.
You'd better bring her in to see me right away.
I can't – she's already flown south for the winter.

Doctor, doctor, I've swallowed a bone.
Are you choking?
No, I'm serious!

Doctor, doctor, I think I'm an elastic band.

Just you stretch out on the couch.

70

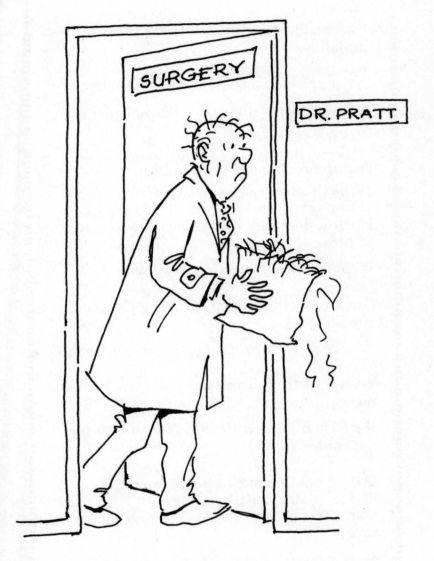

Doctor, doctor, my hair's falling out and I want something to keep it in.

All right, here's a paper bag.

Doctor, doctor, I keep thinking I'm invisible.

I'm sorry, I can't see you now.

Doctor, doctor, I think I'm made of liquorice.

Well it takes all sorts.

Doctor, doctor, I feel like a gherkin.

Oh dear, what a pickle to be in!

Doctor, doctor, I've just swallowed a roll of film.

Well, let's hope nothing develops.

Doctor, doctor, I keep thinking I'm a rubber tyre.

You've got an inflated opinion of yourself!

Waiter, waiter, bring me some tea without milk.

We haven't any milk, sir. How about tea without cream?

Man: What kind of bird is this, waiter?
Waiter: It's a wood pigeon, sir.
Man: I thought so – would you bring me a saw?

Waiter, waiter. This egg tastes rather strong!

Don't worry sir, the tea's rather weak.

Waiter, waiter. Why is this piece of toast all broken?

Well, you did say 'Toast and coffee and step on it'.

Waiter, waiter, I can't eat this meat, it's crawling with maggots.

Don't worry, sir, I'll catch it at the end of the table.

Waiter, waiter, there's a small beetle in my lettuce.

Hang on one moment, sir, I'll see if I can find a larger one.

Waiter, waiter, there's a dead spider in my soup.

Yes, sir, it's the boiling water that kills them.

Waiter, waiter, there's something wrong with these eggs!

Don't blame me, sir, I only laid the table.

Waiter, waiter, this crab's only got one claw.
It's been in a fight, sir.
Then bring me the winner!

Waiter, waiter, is there chocolate mousse on the menu?

No sir, I wiped it off!

Waiter, waiter, will the pancakes be long?

No sir, round.

Customer: There's a fly in my soup.
Waiter: Don't worry, sir – the spider on the bread roll will get him.

Sir Harry Secombe CBE

Waiter, waiter, there's an earwig in my soup.

That's funny. It's usually a fly!

Waiter, waiter, where's my honey?
She left last week, sir!

Waiter, waiter, there's a twig in my soup!
Yes sir, we have branches everywhere.

Waiter, waiter, there's a fly in my soup!
Yes, I know, sir, it's the rotting meat that attracts them.

Waiter, waiter, do you serve crabs?
Take a seat, sir. We serve anybody.

Waiter, waiter, there's another fly in my soup!

It's fly soup, sir!

Waiter, waiter, there are two flies in my soup!

This week's special offer, sir.

Waiter, waiter, there are *five* flies in my soup!

Goodness, sir, one more and you'd have a world record!

Waiter, waiter, there's a cockroach in my soup!

Yes sir, the fly is on holiday!

Waiter, waiter, what's this fly doing in my soup?

Looks like the breast-stroke, sir.

Waiter, waiter, what soup is this?
It's bean soup, sir.
I don't want to know what it's *been*, I want to know what it *is*!

Waiter, waiter, there's a button on my potato.

Well sir, you did ask for a jacket potato.

Waiter, waiter, have you got frog's legs?

No, sir. I always walk like this.

There's a bloke going into Australia as an immigrant, and they said, 'Do you have a police record?' He said, 'I didn't think it was still compulsory.'

Australians are a funny bunch – they always answer their own questions. They say things like, 'What's your favourite colour, blue?', 'What do you do for a living, digger?', 'What's your favourite hobby, sport?', 'What's your girlfriend's name, Sheila?'

Why did the nurse tiptoe past the cupboard?

So she wouldn't wake the sleeping pills.

Why did they use candles in the Middle Ages?

Because it was knight time.

What did the poet say to the rain?

Drop in some time.

Waiter, waiter, I can't eat this chicken. Call the manager.

You are wasting your time, sir, he won't eat it either.

There's the Irishman digging the trench, and the boss came along and said, 'I'm very impressed with this. Honestly, you've done a marvellous job, we're going to get you a JCB.' And the Irish feller said, 'Never mind the medals, just get someone in here to help me.'

Two Irish fellers walked up a street in Canada and they saw a sign saying, 'Tree Fellers Wanted', and they said, 'Look, if Murphy had come we coulda got that job.'

Then there's the Irish feller in the police station and on the wall there are lots of pictures with 'Wanted for Murder', 'Wanted for Robbery', 'Wanted for Assault' on them. He said, 'I can't understand these police, if they want all these fellers why didn't they keep hold of them when they were taking their pictures?'

Teacher: Did you know that people often look like their pets?
Bob: Miss, you don't have a goldfish by any chance, do you?

There are zillions of terrible animal stories, and here's one of my firm favourites. It's the one about the feller whose pal says, 'If you're looking for a job, it's a hundred quid a week, no problems, all you can eat, all you can drink. What's happened is, the monkey's gone ill at the zoo, all you have to do is dress up in a gorilla skin and bounce around the cage, five hours a day throughout the summer.' So they put him in the gorilla skin and he's bouncing around this cage, and he bounces too hard and the floor falls through, dropping him into a cage full of lions. And he starts to scream, and one of the lions says, 'Shut your gob, pal, or you'll get us all the sack.'

What do you call a friendly and handsome monster?

A failure.

COR!

Why did dinosaurs have such long necks?
Because they had smelly feet.

A mother said to her child who was getting on her nerves, 'Make yourself useful, go and give the goldfish some water,' and the child answered, 'I don't see the sense in that, it hasn't drunk the last lot yet.'

Frankie Howerd

Where do tough chickens come from?
Hard boiled eggs.

Did you hear the one about the man who walked into a pub with a baby elephant under his arm? 'Where on earth did you get that thing?' said the barman. 'I won it in a raffle,' said the elephant.

How does a sheep keep warm in winter?
By central bleating.

What's black and white and red all over?
A zebra with sun burn.

There was a magician on board a ship and before every trick he did a parrot in a cage explained to the audience how it was done. He ruined the magician's tricks on five different shows.

One night halfway through a performance, the ship struck an iceberg and went down. The magician was thrown overboard and he ended up on a piece of driftwood, and sitting on the end of the driftwood was the parrot. After two days drifting about at sea the parrot said,

'Okay, wiseguy, what did you do with the ship?'

What goes from green to red at the flick of a switch?
A frog in a blender.

What goes zzub, zzub?
A bee flying backwards.

A man walked into a pub with his pet giraffe.
After a couple of drinks, the giraffe passed out
so the man got fed up and started to leave.
The barman shouted to him, 'You can't leave
that lying there.' The man replied, 'It's not a
lion, it's a giraffe!'

Did you hear the one about the two fleas who won the Pools?
They bought a dog in Spain.

Russ Abbot

A man walked into a pub with a huge, vicious looking Rottweiler. 'I'm sorry, sir,' said the landlord, 'but that dog looks pretty dangerous to me: he might frighten the other customers, so I'm going to have to ask you to leave him outside.' So the man took the dog outside and tied him up, and came back into the pub to enjoy his drink. He was just finishing when a young woman came in and said, 'Whose Rottweiler is that outside?'

'It's mine,' said the proud owner.

'I'm terribly sorry,' said the woman, 'but my dog has just killed him!'

'Killed him!' said the man in disbelief. 'What kind of dog do you have?'

'A Yorkshire terrier,' said the woman.

'How on earth could a little Yorkie kill my enormous Rottweiler?'

'She got stuck in his throat and choked him.'

Why do bees hum?
Because they don't know the words.

What horse never jumps?
A clothes horse.

How do you stop a dog barking in the back seat of your car?
Put him in the front seat.

How many monkeys can you put in an empty telephone box?
One – then it would not be empty.

What do you call a fly with no wings?
A walk!

What do you get if you run over a canary?
Shredded Tweet.

What's big, bright and silly?
A fool moon.

What's furry and minty?
Polo Bear.

What do gorillas sing at Christmas?
Jungle Bells, Jungle Bells.

What year do kangaroos like?
Leap year.

What happened when the dog went to the
flea circus?

He stole the show.

What has four legs and one arm?
A Rottweiler.
Joanna Lumley

What is the difference between an
elephant and a biscuit?
You can't dip an elephant in your tea.

What did the pony say when he coughed?
Excuse me, I'm a little hoarse....

What do you get if you plant a gun?
Lots of little shoots.

What tree never grows?
A shoe tree.

Where was the first potato found?
In the ground.

Why did the chicken cross the road softly?
Because he couldn't walk hardly.

The dentist put his fingers in the crocodile's mouth to see how many teeth it had. What did the crocodile do? It closed its mouth to see how many fingers the dentist had!

How many elephants can you fit in a car?
Two in the front and two in the back.

How many giraffes can you fit in a car?
None, because the elephants are in it already.

What is bright blue and weighs four tonnes?
An elephant holding its breath.

What do cows eat for breakfast?
Moosli.

How does an elephant hide in a cherry tree?

He paints his toe nails red.

Why is an elephant big, grey and wrinkly?

Because if it was small, white and smooth, it would be an aspirin.

Why wouldn't Noah let the two maggots in the apple on the Ark?

Because he only took animals in pears.

How do you know if there is an elephant in your bed.

By the 'E' on his pyjama pockets.

Why did the cowslip?

Because it saw the bulrush.

Why did the dinosaur cross the river?

Because there were no roads in those days.

What do you get if you cross an elephant with a kangaroo?

Holes in Australia.

Why are flowers so lazy?

Because they are always in bed.

How do you tell if there is an elephant
under your bed?

Your nose is touching the ceiling.

A gorilla walked into a pub and ordered a
pint of bitter. The barman served him and
charged him £5.

'Do you know,' said the barman, 'you're
the first gorilla we've had in this bar for
years.'

'At a fiver a pint,' said the gorilla, 'I'm
not surprised.'

Knock, knock.
Who's there?
Witch.
Witch who?
Witch you doing round here?

Knock, knock.
Who's there?
Ida.
Ida who?
Ida better come in, it's raining.

Knock, knock.
Who's there?
Waiter.
Waiter who?

Knock! Knock!

Waiter minute while I tie up my shoe lace.

Knock, knock.
Who's there?
Arthur.
Arthur who?
Arthur any more at home like you?

Knock, knock.
Who's there?
Snow.
Snow who?
Snow use, I've forgotten.

Knock, knock.
Who's there?
Minerva.
Minerva who?
Minerva Zerekt from all these questions.

Why can't penguins fly?
Because they're a chocolate biscuit.

Gary Lineker

Why do elephants have big ears?

Because Noddy wouldn't pay the ransom.

Why did the sparrow fly into the library?

It was looking for bookworms.

What did the zebra say when he crossed the zebra crossing?

'Now you see me, now you don't!'

Why was the crab arrested?

It kept pinching things.

What is white and goes up?

A silly snowflake.

Where do sheep get their hair cut?
At the baa-baa's shop.

What is a duck's favourite television programme?
The feather forecast.

First cow: 'Have you felt any effects of mad cow disease?'
Second cow: 'Don't ask me, I'm a squirrel.'

Baby camel to his mother: 'Mum, why have we got a hump on our back?'
'That's so we can carry water when we go on long journeys across the desert, son.'
Baby camel: 'Why do we have long eyelashes?'
Mother camel: 'They're to protect our eyes against the sandstorms in the desert, son.'
Baby camel: 'And why do we have these huge flat hooves?'
Mother camel: 'So we can walk across the sand dunes without sinking in the sand.'
Baby camel: 'But mum, why are we in London Zoo?'

Why did the cherry go out with the fig?
Because he couldn't find a date.

There was this man who had a dog with no legs. He used to call it Cigarette – 'cos at night time he had to take it out for a drag.

Norman Wisdom

What happened to the frog who broke down on the motorway?

He got toad away.

What did King Kong say when he heard his sister had had a baby?

Well, I'll be a monkey's uncle.

What is a crocodile's favourite drink?

Crocacola.

What do you call an elephant witch doctor?

Mumbo jumbo.

What happened to the man who bought a box of fly killer?

He opened it and found a spider.

What's big and black and hairy and flies to America?

King Concorde.

What will happen when pigs learn to fly?

Bacon will go up in price.

Why are goldfish red?

Because water makes them rusty.

What do you call a dinosaur with one eye?
Do-you-think-he-saw-us.

What's green and goes 'boing, boing'?

A spring cabbage.

Did you hear the one about the Irish turkey that looked forward to Christmas?

What do you call a pig when it's tumbling down a hill?

A sausage roll.

Why do all elephants have the same coloured trunks?

Because they all belong to the same swimming club.

Why did the dinosaur cross the road?

Because chickens weren't invented.

Why did the parrot wear a raincoat?

It wanted to be polly-unsaturated.

What's a shark's favourite meal?

Fish and ships.

What happened to the cat who ate wool?

She had mittens.

When is it bad luck to have a black cat follow you?

When you are a mouse.

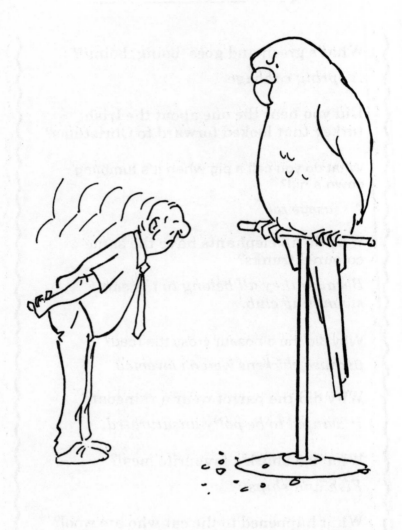

What do you call a nine foot budgie?
Sir.

The Australian cricket team arrived off the ship in Liverpool to play a Test series in England. As the weather was so fine and they were waiting for their luggage they thought why didn't they get a day's practice in. So they went up to the Head Docker and they said, 'Any chance of fielding a cricket team against us? We can play in the dockyard.'

He said, 'We have got quite a few good batters and bowlers, I'll try and round up as many as I can.' He came back and said, 'I've actually got ten, we're one short at the moment but Harry will be along with the horse in a minute, he'll probably play.' So up comes Harry leading this old grey mare. 'Do you fancy turning your arm over against the Aussies?'

Harry said, 'Oh no, my back's gone, I'd be hopeless but the horse will play.'

He said, 'What?'

'The horse will play, it's brilliant.'

So the dockers won the toss and said they'd put the Aussies in first. They bowled a couple of overs and then Harry said to the Captain, 'Give the horse a turn.'

The Captain said, 'Can it bowl?'

'Bowl', he said, 'it's a reborn Freddie Trueman, put the ball in its hoof.' So the horse bowled six balls, and bowled six fellers completely out. The Captain said, 'Can it field?'

'Field, it's the finest slip fielder you have ever seen. Put it in first slip.' So they stood the horse at first slip. It caught the next five balls. So the Aussies were all out for none. 'What about batting?'

'It's the most brilliant batter you have ever seen, put the bat in its hoof, put him in first.' So they put the horse at the wicket with the bat in its hoof. The Aussie bowler came up, bowled the ball at him, the horse smashed it out of sight and the Captain shouted, 'Run!' and Harry said;

'Don't be stupid, if it could run it'd be at Aintree.'

Which bird has no feathers, can't fly and eats eggs?

A jailbird.

What's thick, yellow and dangerous?
Shark-infested custard.

What's brown and has a trunk?

A mouse coming back from holiday.

The world's most valuable Persian cat was stolen. The police were called. After investigating, they called a mews conference.

Why do budgerigars always phone their friends in the evening?

Because it's CHEEP rate after 6pm.

Which animal would you like to be on a cold day?

A little otter.

What should you do if you see a vicious shaggy dog?

Hope he doesn't see you.

What do you get if you cross a chicken with a kangaroo?

Pouched eggs!

What do you get if you cross a cow, a sheep and a baby seal?

The milky bar goat.

What travels along the riverbed at a hundred mph?

A motor pike and side carp.

What do you call a giraffe at the North Pole?
Lost.

What goes 'Croak dot, croak dot, croak dot'?

Morse toad.

What do you get if you cross a lemon with a cat?

A sour puss.

How does an octopus go to war?

Well armed.

What goes 99-bump, 99-bump, 99-bump?

A centipede with a wooden leg.

What kind of doctor treats ducks?

A quack.

What would you get if you crossed a sheep with a kangaroo?

A woolly jumper.

Did you hear about the angry rabbit?

It was hopping mad.

What do you get if you cross a pigeon with a racing tip?

A bird that lays odds.

Speaker A: 'My dog's got no nose.'
Speaker B: 'How does he smell?'
Speaker A: 'Terrible.'

Jimmy Greaves

What do you get if you cross a hedgehog with a giraffe?

A long-necked toothbrush.

Why do horses have hooves?

Because they'd look silly in carpet slippers.

What do you call a cat who has swallowed a duck?

A duck-filled fatty puss.

How to Complain by Mona Lott

How to Make a Fortune by Roy L Mint

How to Decorate Your House by Walter Wall

How to Go Bankrupt by Denis Awlgon

How to Compliment People by Hugh R Loughly

How to Save Souls by Eve Anne Gellist

How to Make Decisions with Confidence by Phyllis Wright

How to Steal Cattle by Russell Steers

How to Invent Things by Chester Nighdear

What do you call a deaf grizzly bear?
Anything you like, it can't hear you.

The lion was walking through the jungle when he met a little mouse.

'Who's the King of the Jungle?' asked the lion.

'You are,' said the little mouse.

'Correct,' said the lion. 'And don't you forget it.'

So saying, he picked the mouse up and threw him against a tree.

A little later the lion met a chimpanzee.

'Who's the King of the Jungle?' asked the lion.

'You are,' said the chimp.

'That's right,' said the lion. 'And don't you forget it.'

So saying, he knocked the chimp down and stamped all over him.

The same thing happened with every animal the lion met.

Finally he met an elephant.

'Who's the King of the Jungle?' asked the lion.

The elephant picked up the lion with his trunk, threw him to the ground, sat on him, picked him up by the tail and battered him against a tree.

The lion staggered to his feet, bruised and bleeding, and said, 'How stupid of me not to recognize you, Your Majesty.'

What's a polygon?
A dead parrot.

What do elephants play in the back of a mini?
Squash.

Why is getting up at three o'clock in the morning like a pig's tail?
Because it's t'wirly.

A white horse walked into a pub and asked for a pint of bitter.
　　The barman said, 'I didn't know you could talk.'
　　And the horse said, 'Oh yes.'
　　'That's a real coincidence, we've got a whisky named after you.'
　　And the horse said, 'Oh really? Percy?'

Why do golfers wear two pairs of trousers?

In case they get a hole in one.

How do you get down from an elephant?

You don't get down from an elephant, you get down from a swan.

What is a myth?

A female moth.

Why do birds have feathers?

Because they'd look silly in trenchcoats.

A duck walked into a shop and asked for a packet of mints.
'That'll be 26 pence,' said the shop assistant.
'Put them on my bill,' said the duck.

Two boy centipedes were standing on the street corner when a girl centipede passed by.
'Look at that!' said one boy centipede admiringly. 'That's what I call a good pair of legs . . . pair of legs . . . pair of legs. . . .'

What do you call the lion that eats its mother's sister?

An aunt-eater.

I once did a tour with a rock band where nobody knew who the heck I was, and all I was doing was wasting time before their favourites came on. That's a *bad* audience! A *good* one is the one who arrives to see you. And even that can be tricky, of course. I've made four or five comedy LPs now, and you get people bringing their families just to hear a specific part of a record, and I'm leaving it out because I'm thinking everyone's heard that now. It can get unnerving because you actually get requests for jokes. Probably one of the most popular ones is the American tourist who went to a dockside café in Liverpool, with forty-eight cameras around his head, and the girl behind the counter, who's lethal, she's got answers to everything. He says, 'This steak's funny.' 'Well laugh at it.' And he says, 'I've come all the way from America and I want a big celebration meal, I want a sheep's head.' And she shouts through the hatch, 'Sheep's head for one.' He says, 'And I want it American style.' She shouts, 'Take the brains out.'

What does a rabbit want to do when he grows up?

He wants to join the Royal Hare Force.

What's yellow and smells of bananas?
Monkey sick.

Cilla Black

What do you call a fish in a cowboy hat?
Billy the Squid.

How do you make a poisonous snake cry?
Take away its rattle.

Where did Noah keep his bees?
In the ark hives.

What's the difference between a lion with toothache and a rainstorm?
One roars with pain, the other pours with rain.

Just before closing time, a flea dashed into a pub, ordered five double whiskys, drank them straight down, rushed into the street, jumped high in the air and fell flat on his face.

'Damn it!' he cried as he picked himself up, 'Who's moved my dog?'

What comes out of a wardrobe at 100mph?

Stirling Moth.

What do you call the dog that composed *Madame Butterfly*?

Poochini.

What do you get if you cross a parrot with a woodpecker?

A bird that talks in Morse code.

How do you stop a cockerel crowing on Monday morning?

Have him for lunch on Sunday.

What is the difference between a jogging rabbit and a rabbit with a flower up its nose?

One is a fit bunny and the other is a bit funny.

When is a car like a frog?

When it's being toad.

What do you do with a cat that's lost its tail?

Take it to the retail shop.

A baby bear went to see his dad, sitting on the ice floes. He said to him, 'Dad, am I a polar bear?'

And his dad said, 'Yes, son, you are.'

'I mean, I am a real polar bear, aren't I?' said baby bear, 'a really, really, truly, truly, polar-beary polar bear?'

'But of course you are, son,' said his dad. 'Of course you are.'

'One hundred per cent?'

'Yes, one hundred per cent.'

'Well in that case, why am I so cold?'

What do you call a woodpecker with no beak?

A headbanger.

Did you hear about the prawn that went to a cocktail party?

He pulled a mussel.

Did you hear about the monster with the sore throat?

He spent all day gargoyling.

What fish are other fish most frightened of?

Jack the Kipper.

Why do elephants have flat feet?

From jumping out of tall trees.

I suppose if you were to stand all the great comics in a line, my number one favourite would be Al Read. He was the first, and probably the best exponent of looking at life, a man who could draw a picture in one sentence. The lovely line of the wife saying to her husband 'That's an awful lot of after-shave for a darts match.' That's brilliant, it says it all in one go.

Tommy Cooper was another favourite. He used to do that one where a feller jumped in the back of a taxi and said, 'King Arthur's Close', and the taxi driver says, 'Don't worry, I'll lose him at the next set of lights.'

There's a lovely joke always attributed to Dave Allen, about the fellow on the building site up on the top floor, and the boss down below shouting, 'You, you're fired, get your cards.' The bloke shouted, 'What?' He said, 'You up there, you're fired, get your cards.' The feller said, 'What?' The boss said, 'Oh forget it, I'll sack somebody else.' And the bloke at the top of the building said, 'You do that and we'll have the union on you.'

That reminds me of a nice story by George Roper, on *The Comedians*, about the feller

120

digging a hole, and the boss comes up and says, 'This isn't going at all well. Everybody get out of the hole.' So they all get out of the hole. And he says, 'Right, stamp your feet.' So they all stamp their feet. He says, 'Jump back in.' They jump back in. He says, 'Jump out and stamp your feet again.' They say, 'Why are we doing this?' He says, 'You're bringing more muck out on your shoes than you were on your shovels.'

What goes Peck Peck Bang, Peck Peck Bang, Peck Peck Bang?

A chicken in a minefield.

When will a cat not enter a house?

When the door is closed.

How do you get two elephants in a match box?

Take out the matches first.

There were two lions walking down Brighton pier. One said to the other, 'It's quiet for a bank holiday.'

A lion went into a shop and said, 'I'd like a fur coat.'
 They said, 'And why on earth do you want a fur coat?'
 He said, 'I'd look a fool in a plastic mac.'

What do you get if you cross an elephant
with a mouse?

Huge holes in the skirting-boards.

Here's my all-time favourite gag – I don't know why.

There are three cross-eyed witnesses in the box and a cross-eyed judge, and the judge says to the first accused, 'Do you plead guilty or not guilty?' And the second feller says, 'Not guilty'. The judge says, 'I wasn't speaking to you.' And the third feller says, 'I didn't even open my mouth.'

And here are loads more, worse than that!

What do you call a girl standing in the middle of a tennis court?

Annette.

What did one eye say to the other eye?

Something's come between us and it smells.

What do you call a man who inspects rabbit holes?

A borough surveyor.

Knock! Knock!

Knock, knock.

Who's there?

Orson.

Orson who?

Orson cart.

Knock, knock.

Who's there?

Didi.

Didi who?

Didi cow jump over the moon?

Knock, knock.

Who's there?

Aida.

Aida who?

Aida a big breakfast before coming to work!

Knock, knock.

Who's there?

Justin.

Justin who?

Justin time for a cup of tea.

Knock, knock.

Who's there?

Dunce.

Dunce who?

Dunce A another word.

Knock, knock.

Who's there?

Dawn.

Dawn who?

Dawn do anything I wouldn't do.

Knock, knock.

Who's there?

Yah.

Yah who?

Ride 'em, Cowboy!

What is an 'ig'?
An Eskimo's house without a toilet.

What did one tonsil say to the other tonsil?

You'd better get dressed, the doctor is taking us out tonight.

What gets wetter as it dries?

A towel.

Why is Wales slowly sinking into the sea?

Too many leeks.

What is easy to get into but difficult to get out of?

Trouble.

How do you make a bandstand?

Hide all the chairs.

What did the sea say to the sand?

Nothing, it just waved.

Why are Saturday and Sunday strong days?

Because the rest are 'week days'.

What travels around the world yet stays in one corner?

A postage stamp.

The preparations were going on the day
before the Battle of Hastings and King
Harold was going out to survey his troops.
The General said, 'Here look at this.
Spearmen, fire', and the fellers with spears
flung them in the air and they all landed
accurately around the target. The King said,
'That's tremendous.'

'Swordsmen, present arms,' said the
General, and all the fellers whipped their
swords out from the scabbards and thrust
them in the air with gay abandon, and the
King said, 'That's brilliant.'

The General said, 'Right, archers, fire.'
They all fired and one bloke let loose an
arrow and it went up, it got about half a
mile, turned round in a complete circle, like
a boomerang, and came back over their
heads. And King Harold said, 'General,
you'll have to watch that feller tomorrow –
he'll have somebody's eye out.'

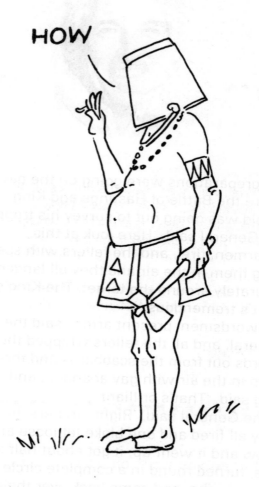

Why did the Indian have a bucket on his head?

Because he was a pale face.

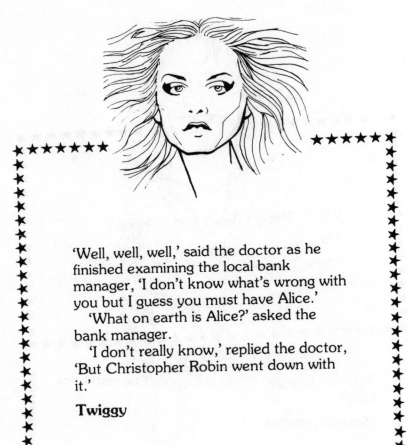

'Well, well, well,' said the doctor as he finished examining the local bank manager, 'I don't know what's wrong with you but I guess you must have Alice.'

'What on earth is Alice?' asked the bank manager.

'I don't really know,' replied the doctor, 'But Christopher Robin went down with it.'

Twiggy

What do you write on a robot's grave?

Rust in Peace.

What did the scarf say to the hat?

You go on ahead and I'll hang around here.

What's Rupert Bear's middle name?

The.

Chris Tarrant

What do you get if you step on a Spanish bank note?

Mashed pesetas.

Why is six afraid of seven?

Because seven ate nine.

Why did Cinderella get thrown out of the football team?

Because she kept on running away from the ball.

Do robots have brothers?

No, only transistors!

What bus has sailed the ocean?

Columbus has, of course.

What's the difference between an angry rabbit and a counterfeit ten pound note?

One's a mad bunny and the other's bad money.

What's small and green and travels at 80mph?

An MG Midget Sprout.

What's worse than being with a fool?

Fooling with a bee.

What do you call a boomerang that doesn't come back?

A stick.

What always weighs the same, no matter how big it gets?

A hole.

Why is a ship called a She?

Because it hangs around buoys.

What do you call a bull sleeping on the ground?

A bull dozer.

What is green, has six legs and if it fell
out of a tree would kill you?

A snooker table.

A feller wanted to buy a new car in Moscow. The dealer said, 'You understand that there is a huge waiting list for them?'

'I don't mind,' said the man, 'I want to put my name down.'

'It will be 27 years from today.'

The bloke said, 'Is that exact?'

He said, 'Yes, exactly 27 years from today you will have your new car.'

The feller said, 'Will that be morning or afternoon?'

The dealer said, 'What?'

He said, 'Well I've got the plumber coming in the morning!'

Which month has twenty-eight days?

All of them.

Where's Yarmouth?

Under Yar Nose.

What's the longest word in the world?
Smiles – there's a mile between the first
S and the last S.

Richard Branson

What do you get if you cross a giraffe with a toothbrush?

A very tall toothbrush.

What do you call two banana skins?

A pair of slippers.

'Have I told you the one about the wall?'
'No'
'I'd better not tell you, you'll never get over it!'

Who can jump higher than a house?

Anyone, a house can't jump.

What do you call a nun with a washing machine?

Sistermatic.

What did the robot say to the petrol pump?

Take your finger out of your ear when I'm talking to you.

Why is it dangerous to sleep in a train?

Because trains run over sleepers.

What do you get if you cross a football team with a big tub of ice cream?

Aston Vanilla.

Where does Thursday come before Wednesday?

In a dictionary.

Why do Skodas have heated rear windscreens?

To keep your hands warm while you're pushing it.

Instructor: Well, son, it's about time you took your first parachute jump.
Pupil: But what happens if the parachute doesn't open?
Instructor: If that happens, you'll find yourself jumping to a conclusion.

Here's a story about Howard Hughes.

Wherever he went in the world on holiday, he did not just rent an hotel, he bought it and the story goes that he was looking at this place in Florida for a holiday and down came his men and they buy the hotel. They said, 'Let's have a look at the royalty suite.' They got into the royalty suite and looked out of the window and they said, 'Yes, beautiful room. The only trouble is the view is wrong.'

The Manager said, 'What's wrong with the view?'

'Well, for a start the beach, the beach is pebbly, it should have sand.'

He said, 'We'll bring some tankers down and tip sand all over the place and make it nice and yellow.' With that of course came thousands of these tanker trucks with this yellow sand so that was that.

Then they said, 'The sea is the wrong colour.'

The Manager said, 'The sea?'

They said, 'It's too green, he wants a nice blue sea.'

So out came some oil tankers with some special dye and they blue the sea up.

Then they said, 'The sky has got to go.'

And the Manager said, 'Don't be daft.'

'It's too cloudy, we want a clear blue sky.' So over came these huge jet planes and they dropped cubes of ice which dispersed all the clouds. About two hours later, Howard Hughes arrived at the hotel and he walked upstairs into the royalty suite. Went to the window, looked out and said, 'Everywhere you go is the same isn't it?'

What's the easiest way to rob a bank?

Do a safe robbery.

What would you do if you broke your leg in three places?

You'd never return to those three places!

What has eight feet and sings?

A quartet.

What do you get if you cross the Atlantic with the *Titanic?*

Halfway.

What do short-sighted ghosts wear?
Spooktacles.

★★★★★★★★★★★ ★★★★★★★★★★★★

Which two words have the most letters?
Post Office.

Anthony Andrews

★★★★★★★★★★★★★★★★★★★★★★★★

What did John McEnroe say when he saw the
Dog Star through his telescope?
That cannot be Sirius.

What do you call a Skoda with a sunshine
roof?
A skip.

Did you know you can now get microwave
beds? You get eight hours sleep in just ten
minutes.

A chap walked into a Skoda distributor's.
'Will you give me a wing mirror for my
Skoda?'
'Yes, that's a fair exchange!'

I'm often asked why so many comedians come from Liverpool. There are several old chestnuts on this one. One is that you've got to be a comedian to live there. I don't believe that. I agree with the late Arthur Askey in as much as comedians generally come from the great cosmopolitan areas, and generally you find that in the early days they came from areas that were very deprived – the theory being that to prove you are not afraid of things, you laugh at them. And also, of course, in Liverpool they say you've got nothing to lose so you might as well make fun of it anyway!

Why did the skeleton climb a tree?

Because a dog was after its bones.

What runs around the garden but never moves?

A fence.

Why did the Romans build straight roads?

So they wouldn't go round the bend.

What lives at the bottom of the sea and shivers?

A nervous wreck.

Why did the sieve retire?

It couldn't take the strain.

Did you hear the one about the man who invented the door knocker?

He won the no-bell prize.

Who built the first plane which did not fly?

The wrong brothers.

What did the Pink Panther say when he stepped on an ant?
 '*Dead ant, dead ant, dead ant dead ant dead ant . . . !*'
 (To the tune of *Pink Panther*).
Anton Rodgers

When the soldiers got back to England, after the retreat from Dunkirk, they had lost all their belongings. The Sergeant said to one, 'Where's your rifle?'

He said, 'I lost it, Sir, when we were boarding the ship, we were under heavy gunfire, and the Luftwaffe were strafing us. I am sorry, it fell in the sea and I had to save myself.'

The Sergeant said, 'Listen, pal, it doesn't matter what the conditions were, you've lost your rifle, it was the King's property, and I am afraid you are going to have to pay for it.'

'I have got to pay for my rifle?'

The Sergeant said, 'Yes.'

'Do you mean if I had been a tank driver and I had abandoned my tank, I would have had to pay for that?'

The Sergeant said, 'Yes.'

He said, 'My God, no wonder these Captains go down with their ships.'

The Pestalozzi Children's Village

The aim of the Pestalozzi Children's Village is to give the brightest children from the poorest areas of the world the best education and practical training available so they can return home and help build a better future. Today, more than 120 Indian, Thai, Tibetan, Nepalese and Zambian children live in the village based around a working farm in the Sussex countryside. They are high-ability children with no hope of secondary education in their own countries. Each child is carefully chosen from stable families living in poor rural areas and, with the agreement of their parents, they come to England aged ten, just as their normal schooling is coming to an end. They live at the Pestalozzi Village in 'national' families, with housemothers from their own country who help them to continue to learn about their own culture, language and religion.

Dozens of Pestalozzi students have already completed their training and have returned home as engineers, agriculturalists, managers, teachers, nurses, technologists and craftsmen. Today they are sharing their knowledge to help the sustainable development of their own countries.

For more information about the Pestalozzi Children's Village please contact:

The Appeals Department
Pestalozzi Children's Village Trust
Sedlescombe
Battle
East Sussex TN33 0RR
Telephone: (0424) 870444